The TA Primer

the TA primer

Transactional Analysis in Everyday Life

ADELAIDE BRY, M.Ed.

Photographs and drawings by
Karen Schwoerer

PERENNIAL LIBRARY
Harper & Row, Publishers, Inc.
New York   Evanston   San Francisco   London

THE TA PRIMER: TRANSACTIONAL ANALYSIS IN EVERYDAY LIFE.

Copyright © 1973 by Adelaide Bry
All rights reserved. Printed in the United States of America. No part of this book may be used or reproduced in any manner without written permission except in the case of brief quotations embodied in critical articles and reviews. For information address Harper & Row, Publishers, Inc., 10 East 53rd Street, New York, N.Y. 10022. Published simultaneously in Canada by Fitzhenry & Whiteside Limited, Toronto.

First PERENNIAL LIBRARY edition published 1973.

LIBRARY OF CONGRESS CATALOG CARD NUMBER: 73–3833

STANDARD BOOK NUMBER: 06–080297–9

The TA Primer

Introduction

The TA Primer is your first step toward feeling I'm OK, you're OK.

No matter how young or old you are, you can learn to spot the not-OK feelings inside of you, and then you will be able to learn better ways of feeling that will make your life happier.

You will find out how to understand other people, too.

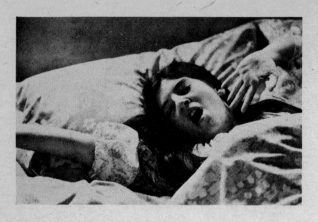

First let's find out something about you. This is you beginning a day. It's a brand new day. What are you feeling?

Do you feel glad to be awake and alive? Are you looking forward to the good things that can happen to you today?

Or . . . is it a bad morning? Do you feel
you don't even want to get up? Do you
begin your day thinking about yourself
and other people in a

     hating
     sad
     angry

way?

If you wake up many mornings feeling sad or angry or just plain miserable, odds are you don't like yourself much. Happy people feel OK about themselves.

And you weren't born feeling miserable.

I'm OK,
You're OK.

The best way you can feel is I'm OK, you're OK. This means you like yourself and other people, too. This means you use your happy feelings to love others, to get your work done, to have a good time. It doesn't mean you think the world is rosy or perfect; you know there are a lot of problems—every day—but you still enjoy living.

Blaming your feelings on other people or on the weather doesn't help you. Sure, sometimes you feel especially happy on a beautiful sunny day, but you can feel OK on the rainiest day.

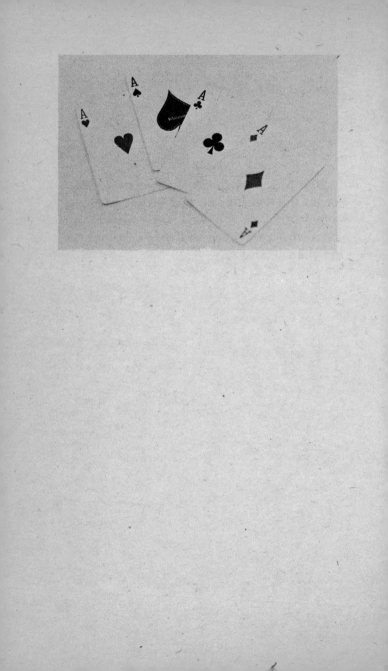

Some people even think that luck will change their feelings.

"If only," they say, "I win at cards or hit the lottery, then I would be happy."

Just excuses.

The very first step toward changing
your feelings is understanding them.
You have inside of you three buttons,
there all the time, waiting to be pushed.
These are called the PAC buttons.

> P stands for parent.
> A stands for adult.
> C stands for child.

(P) ——→ Parent

(A) ——→ Adult

(C) ——→ Child

You have your own idea about what parent, adult, and child mean.

Now you can find out what parent, adult, and child mean in the PAC button language.

The P in the PAC buttons is the parent in you.

P is you behaving and feeling in the very same manner your mother and father behaved and felt. (It could be your aunt or uncle or whoever brought you up. These are your parents in the PAC button language.)

P is the part of you that is both critical and helping or just one or the other.

P is some of your feelings about sex, food, and religion.

P is the "mothering" part of you when you take care of someone.

P is being opinionated, knowing it all.

P is you copying what your parents did (even though you may think you're not and even though you are now twenty-five or forty or even sixty years old).

You *Can't* do it.

When you give someone a "piece of your mind," you're doing just what your parents did to you when you were a child.

Parents use words like

silly
stupid
childish
bad

Parents have been known to say:

You can't win.
Give up.
I know, I've lived longer than you.

Messages from your parents are in your head, no matter how old you are and regardless of whether you remember exactly what they said. These messages are left over from your childhood.

P.S. Some of the messages your parents gave you may be out of date!

Ⓟ Parents are
Ⓐ heavy sometimes
Ⓒ

All parents are heavy sometimes;
parents need to be bossy sometimes, to
tell you what to do and what not to do, to
keep you out of danger.

But some parents are more opinionated
than is necessary; some parents even take
away your fun feelings if they are too
heavy too often.

Does anyone point at you critically and
make you feel small? That person is
behaving like a parent, and making you
feel like a child, the naughty child that
mother or father sent to his room
(sometimes fairly, sometimes not).

If one or both of your parents made you
feel this way often (after all, every child
gets punished once in a while), then you
today are more faultfinding than helpful,
more scolding than loving to others.

Even worse, you're not a KIND
PARENT TO YOURSELF. That comes
first; and if you have children, you may
not be very kind to them.

A happy child has a loving, accepting parent, radiating warmth and approval.

If you got good, warm parenting, you can be a good parent to others or to yourself. (Being a good parent doesn't mean just being a real parent. It means helping others when they need it, acting like a good parent.)

The judgmental, opinionated parent part of you sticks like glue unless you decide you want to change it. How? By pushing the middle PAC button, the A button.

The middle button is the adult button. It's the part of you that asks the question: Does it work? (And "it" means anything in the world you need to make a decision about.)

The adult button in you works like a computer; it stores and collects information about everything. When you need to, you push the adult button to solve problems.

The adult part of you is not emotional.
The adult part of you does not get angry.
The adult part of you makes decisions
based on information.

Some adult words are

>   practical
>   predictable
>   workable
>   manageable

The adult part of you is a
looking-in-the-mirror part. You see
yourself objectively. You *think* about
things before you make up your mind.
   You may be deciding

   whether to move
   what college is right for you
   how you can get along better with
      someone at home or in the office
   why you've been losing your
      temper a lot lately, and how you
      can deal with it

While you're deciding anything, you
don't laugh, you don't cry, you don't get
angry. You put your feelings away.

You don't have to be grownup in years to have an adult. All children have an adult button. Not all parents permit children to push their adult buttons. When parents do, their children grow up independent and able to run their lives successfully. Children need to begin using their adult buttons when they are young in order to get the practice of what it is to make decisions.

A child's adult button is being pushed when she says, "Now it's time to go home for dinner."

A grownup's adult works exactly the same. The adult in you makes the decision that *all* human life is important; this way you feel that you're OK, and other people are, too.

When those not-OK feelings overwhelm you, you push your adult button, and ask yourself, "What happened to me when I was small to make me feel not-OK?" "I know I don't have to feel this way today." Then you turn off the old not-OK messages. The adult in you has to work at this. You've been the other way a long, long time.

P → Parent

A → Adult

C → Child

The third button of the PAC buttons is the child button.

The child is the part of you from your own childhood, the feelings you had when you were three, four, and five years old.

The child is the happy part you need to have all your life. The child button is pushed (no matter how old you are) when you laugh at parties, make up surprises, enjoy sex, cook steak over an open fire, walk in the woods. The child wants to be cared for, loved, and cherished, and the child part returns that love, too. The child button needs to be pushed to put happiness in your life.

There is, too, the sad child part of you; if you were a child who didn't have much fun, you might actually need to push your adult button to give your child permission to laugh and enjoy.

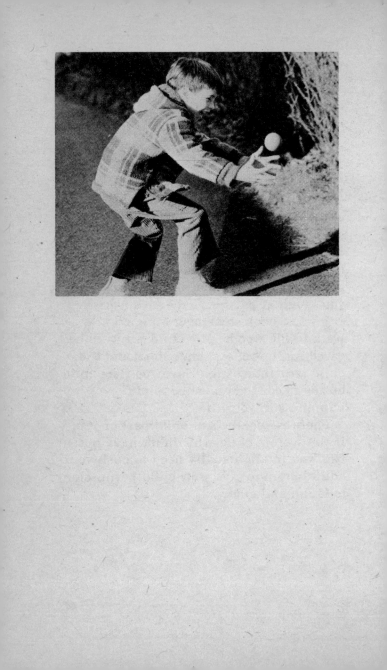

Some grownups have a wonderful happy kid inside; they play and laugh and love, and other people, big and small, like to be around a grownup who feels this way.

Some grownups are unhappy, angry children, kicking and screaming. A little child who doesn't have any fun and isn't allowed to express himself in happy ways is the child who breaks windows or lies. When the child is all grown up he or she does the same kinds of things in grownup ways, such as becoming an alcoholic or being depressed all the time.

When you feel alone and neglected, that is the sad child inside of you. When you push the child button, you may be pushing the happy, creative part of you, or you may be pushing the unhappy, miserable feelings of that little kid.

I don't
Feel good
most of the time.

How do you use the PAC buttons?
Just to say, "I feel good most of the time?"
No. Be a logical adult all the time and
make correct decisions? No. Spend your
whole life as a happy child? No. Act
responsible like a good mother or father?
No.

The way to use the PAC buttons is to
push the right button at the right time.
You need all your PAC buttons in good
working order to make your life work
well for you.

P → Parent

A → Adult

C → Child

You have three buttons inside of you.
The other person does, too. Just like you.

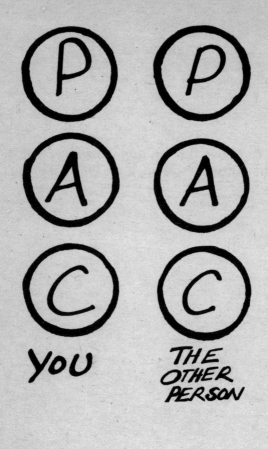

YOU

THE OTHER PERSON

When you communicate with someone else, his PAC buttons and your PAC buttons are *transacting*.

All human beings

    young and old
    rich and poor
    black and white
    men and women
    boys and girls

have PAC buttons.

Transactional Analysis?
What's that?

The proper name to use when you're talking about pushing the PAC buttons is transactional analysis. It's called TA for short.

You can see already it's not even as complicated as this.

A transaction takes place whenever you are involved with someone else, human or animal. When you hug your dog, and he licks your hand, that's a transaction.

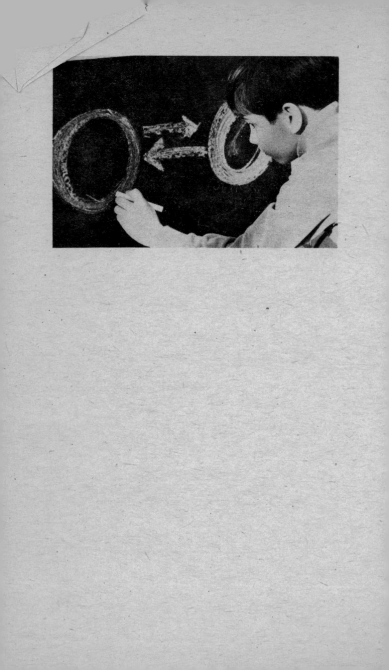

Grownups never studied transactions in school. And neither do children today. You don't learn why you have different kinds of feelings, unfortunately. Feelings are certainly as important as math or science, if not more so.

Don't worry, you won't become a robot when you use TA. But sometimes people say, "I wish I didn't know so much. I'd be happier." Not so. Ignorance about your feelings, about your relationships is seldom bliss. Usually it's just the opposite. Trouble.

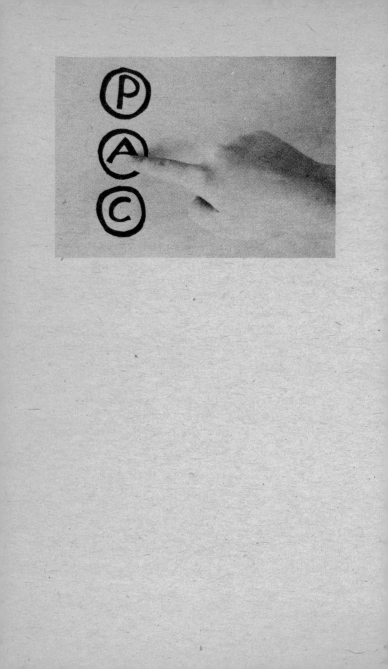

The key to feeling I'm OK, you're OK is
to learn more about yourself and your
relationships by pushing your adult
button. Use your logic. Get unemotional.
When your adult is in full force watch

> the feelings you have in your
>   parent and child
> the way you act in your parent and
>   child
> how other people treat you in your
>   parent and child

Whenever you need to figure *anything*
out, you push your adult button.

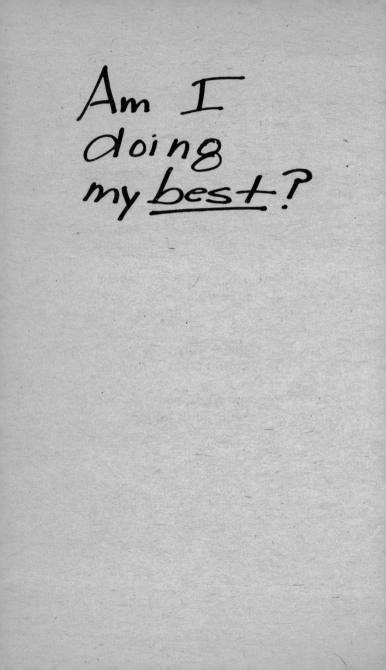

With your adult button pushed in all the way you can ask yourself, "Which part of me am I using now, and am I really doing the best I can?"

After you have solved your problem
(whatever it is), then you are free once
again to be a happy, carefree child
(whether you are ten or seventy).

The goal is to have all the fun you can,
but you must know when. You *always*
have the right to run on the beach, dance,
have OK child fun. (Although some
people think being grownup and being
mature means being stodgy and serious.)

I think you're great.
I like you, too.

In TA language when you say, "I think you're great," and someone says, "I like you, too," you are communicating happy child to happy child.

(If you feel you've lost the ability to be happy, to smell something delicious, to hear the birds, to feel the wind, you can find it again in your happy child.)

This is child to child, a transaction of two happy people communicating.

It's time to leave, now.

Ok, let's go.

Your adult to adult communication on simple things saves you from wasting your emotions, like arguing about when to leave.

Some people are angry children in a conversation about when to leave.

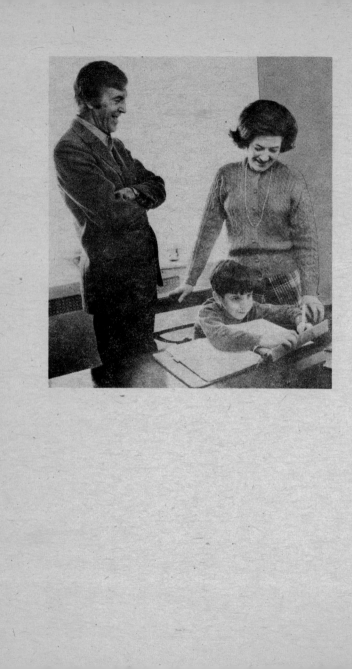

It's fun sometimes to talk parent to parent. They have both pushed their parent buttons and are sharing parental feelings about their child.

When any two people get together and
talk

        parent to parent
        adult to adult
        child to child

that's communicating by pushing the
same button, and it's a good
transaction.
   (It doesn't matter what your age is.)

You can still enjoy a good transaction

when you push	the other person pushes
child	parent
parent	child
adult	child
child	adult
adult	parent
parent	adult

The rule: All combinations are possible; push any button you wish and communicate. (That goes for the other person too.)

But . . . when you say

> "She doesn't understand me."
> "Nobody listens to me."
> "We just can't communicate any
>   more."

you or the other person or maybe both of
you are so busy pushing your own buttons
that communication breaks down.

Watch for the times when you or the
other person gets angry, or hurt, or even
changes the subject. Someone doesn't like
what's being said. Someone doesn't *want*
to listen.

When a man and woman are fighting, it all too often happens that the parent in either one is coming on strong, trying to be the big boss, and making the other into a bad child. He's saying to her,"You're supposed to do it, not me."

But here the woman just refuses to be the bad child. Instead she gets angry and screams, "It's your job."

Now the screaming is louder. Communication has stopped. He pushed the parent button, putting her in the child. But she refused to be the child. And that's a crossed transaction.

Look for a crossed transaction when one person doesn't answer the other but switches the subject. At a movie theater, the ticket man asks, "May I see your ticket?" The customer answers angrily, "You know I've paid." The correct answer is, "Here's my ticket."

STROKES

Angry transactions turn people away from you. Communication that works (**good** transactions) brings you more *strokes*.

"Strokes" is a TA word which means getting love and good feelings from other people. Everyone can get strokes.

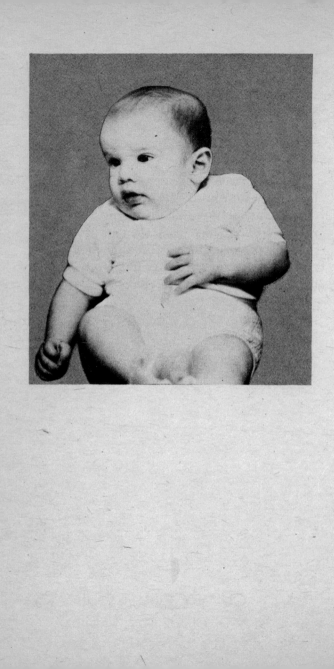

Babies need physical stroking, being held and cuddled. The best stroking is feeling that from the moment you were born you were loved and accepted, just because you're you.

As you get older, you don't need so much cuddling. But you always need someone who cares about you and tells you so. But any attention from another person is a stroke. Even when someone tells you she or he *doesn't* like you.

Lots of parents give their children conditional stroking. They say I'll love you *if*

If you get all *A*s
If you keep your room clean
If you're good
If you make lots of money
If you don't bother me
If you marry the (boy, girl) I want you to

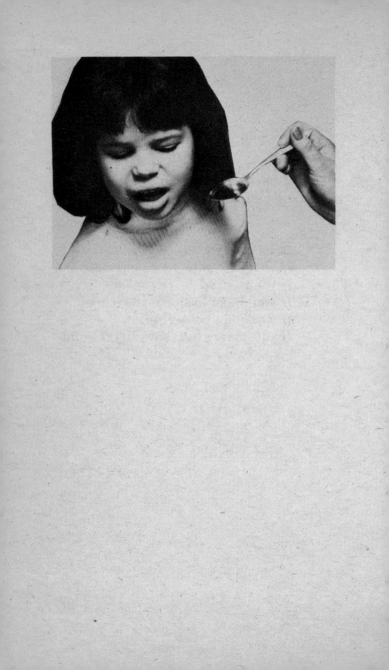

Some parents add a negative *if*.

>I won't love you *if* you don't take
> your medicine.
>I won't love you *if* you don't
> practice your music.

You can always tell a conditional stroke
because it has an *if* in it.

I love you

~~I hate you~~

I HATE YOU—that's a negative stroke
I LOVE YOU—that's a positive stroke.
Both are unconditional strokes.
There's no *if*.

strokes *strokes*
strokes *strokes*
strokes *strokes*
strokes *strokes*
strokes *strokes*
strokes

You need strokes to survive.
Food and water are not enough.
It's better when someone pays attention to you, even if you get spanked or you fight.
Much better than being ignored.
Whether someone listens to you, pats you on the back, or says you're a pain in the ass, it's still stroking.

I'm OK,
You're OK.

To survive you need any kind of strokes, good or bad or even conditional. To feel the best way, I'm OK, you're OK, you need good strokes.

Positive strokes.

Loving strokes.

If you don't get enough good strokes, how can you change this?

How can I
get more <u>strokes</u>?

No matter how old or how young you are right now, ask yourself, "How can I get more strokes?" By pushing the right

P
A
C

button at the right time so that you get good responses from others.

A happy child always gets lots of strokes. A happy child inside the grownup gets lots of strokes, too.

When you're depressed and sad, feeling lonely, you're not getting enough good strokes. And when you do feel and act sad, it keeps you from getting good strokes. Maybe you feel you can't win, that no one cares.

These sad feelings must be just the same lonely feelings you had as a child. But just because you didn't get enough good stroking when you were little doesn't mean you can't change now.

I'm not OK,
You're OK.

In TA talk you're saying you don't feel good enough for the rest of the world. You're saying, "I'm not OK, but everyone else is." Are you getting negative strokes? Are you being ignored?

I'm OK,
You're not OK.

If you got too many mean, angry strokes, you feel alone and distrustful of others. Then you feel, "I'm OK, but you're not OK." Then you say to yourself, "I'm OK, but the world is rotten."

Life
is
Rotten.

When you say, "Life is rotten," you don't win the love and good feelings you need from others.

I'm OK, You're OK

I'm ok, you're not ok.
I'm not ok, you're ok.
I'm not ok, you're not ok.

In this new TA language there are four different ways of feeling about yourself and about other people. Which one describes you?

> I'm OK, you're OK
> I'm OK, you're not OK
> I'm not OK, you're OK
> I'm not OK, you're not OK
>> (if you feel this way, it's the most futile feeling of all, and you have a lot of work to do, using your adult)

I'm pushing my
Adult button
and Listening to
the Kid inside of me.

You will feel I'm OK, you're OK

    as you begin to push your adult
      button regularly
    as you recognize the parts of you
      which don't work very well
    and you see the parts of you that
      need changing
    when you really listen to other
      people of all ages
    when you clear away the
      repetitious messages and listen
      to yourself

You will get more strokes.

Am I good
to myself?

You can be a good parent to *yourself* by not putting yourself down, by loving yourself because you're human, by pushing your adult button to find out how much opinionated parent is left inside of you.

When you begin to love yourself, you'll be able to be a kind parent to everyone from the boss in your office to a friend you see every day.

As you practice giving a smile, approval to young and old, with your parent button pushed, you will be using the parent part you want to keep—regardless of your age.

The judgmental, opinionated parent part of you will take a back seat.

Push your adult button when you find yourself being overbearing, too critical, or just mean and nasty. (That's your hard parent.)

Pulling strings, turning other people into puppets to get what you want won't bring you I'm OK feelings, even though you may win the thing you think you want.

Your goal is to think at the proper
times so that you have

>the freedom to savor your life
>the touch of a hand that you love
>the free, happy laughter from your
>   gut of a funny moment
>the wonder of a leaf turning in the
>   wind

When your adult button is pushed your
computer will start working. Ask yourself

>Is what I want true for me today?
>Are my unhappy child feelings
>   real today?
>Is my adult in proper working
>   order?
>Do I have enough control to count
>   to ten without saying the mean
>   and cruel?
>Do I listen enough to hear what
>   someone else is saying so that I
>   can decide whether it's true or
>   false for me?

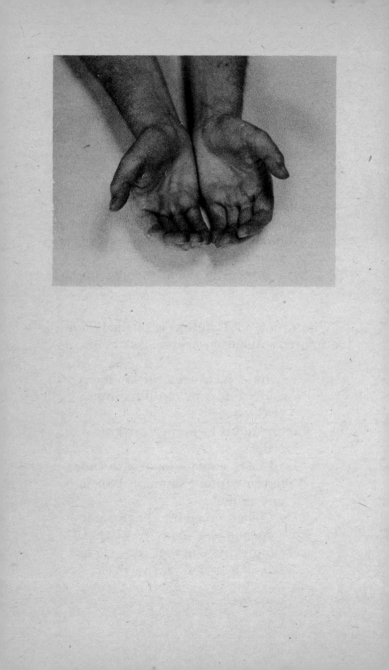

When you believe in TA, when you practice pushing the PAC buttons, You have a new feeling inside. You feel you control your own life. Your life is in *your* hands. You are not destined to do the wrong thing because your mother or father or Uncle Charlie messed up his or her life.

In the beginning as you begin to push your PAC buttons, all kinds of messages will pop into your head.

In using TA you knock on the door of your adult, choosing values and feelings that will make your life happier. When you feel OK, the other people in your life will feel better, too.

Your Life is *your* book and you can rewrite the story of your life. You will have more opportunities to love and do what you really want to do when you know how and why you use your parent, adult, and child buttons every day.

The most important thing to remember is, it's how you feel about yourself that you radiate to others. You weren't born feeling not-OK, and if you feel that way today that's the book you've written—until now.

About the Author

Adelaide Bry is a counseling psychologist in private practice. She is the author of *Inside Psychotherapy* (New York: Basic Books, Inc., 1972) and numerous articles of psychological interest. She uses transactional analysis with groups, and the idea for *The TA Primer* evolved from her need to give people a simple, understandable introduction to the subject.

She is the mother of two children: Barbara, twenty-three, a University of Pennsylvania graduate, and Douglas, twenty, a sophomore at Beloit College. Ms. Bry lectures widely on therapy and has been a guest on the Mike Douglas and Johnny Carson TV programs.